www.raintreepublishers.co.uk
Visit our website to find out
more information about
Raintree books.

To order:

☎ Phone 0845 6044371
🖹 Fax +44 (0) 1865 312263
🖥 Email myorders@raintreepublishers.co.uk

Customers from outside the UK please telephone +44 1865 312262

Raintree is an imprint of Capstone Global Library Limited,
a company incorporated in England and Wales having its
registered office at 7 Pilgrim Street, London, EC4V 6LB –
Registered company number: 6695582

Text © Capstone Global Library Limited 2011
First published in hardback in 2011
The moral rights of the proprietor have been asserted.

Edited by Megan Cotugno
Designed by Ryan Frieson
Original illustrations © Capstone Global Library, Ltd.
Illustrated by Planman Technologies
Picture research by Mica Brancic
Originated by Capstone Global Library, Ltd.
Printed and bound in China by Leo Paper Products Ltd.

ISBN 978 1 4062 2170 1
15 14 13 12 11
11 10 9 8 7 6 5 4 3 2 1

British Library Cataloguing in Publication Data
Fay, Gail.
  Economies around the world. -- (Understanding money)
  1. Economics--Juvenile literature.
  I. Title II. Series
  330.9-dc22

Acknowledgements

The author and publishers are grateful to the following for
permission to reproduce copyright material:

Alamy pp. 27 (© Kevin Foy), 35 (© Paul Maguire), 37 (© Owe
Andersson), 31 (© Megapress); AP/Press Association Images
p. 32 (Ariana Cubillos); Corbis pp. 4 (© Jim Richardson), 8
(Hemis/© Rene Mattes, 10 (epa/© Claudio Peri), 25 (© Alain
Nogues), 39 (© Yann Arthus-Bertrand); Corbis SABA p. 21 (©
Shepard Sherbell); ebay p. 14; Getty Images p. 15 (Washington
Post/James A. Parcell); iStockphoto.com pp. 42 top (©
Ranplett), 42 middle (© Ufuk Zivana), 43 right (© Joe Gough),
43 left (© Brandon Jennings), 42 bottom (© Joe Gough), 13
top (© Pawel Gaul), 18 (© Andy Dean), 13 bottom (© Andrey
Burmakin); Reuters pp. 40 (© Jeff Xu), 29 (© Reinhard
Krause); Shutterstock pp. 5 (© Bartlomiej Magierowski), 6
(© Jo Chambers), 16 (© Perfect Illusion), 28, 23 (© Ragne
Kabanova)

Cover photograph of Shanghai Skyscraper reproduced with
permission of iStockphoto.com (© Nikada).

We would like to thank Michael Miller for his invaluable help
in the preparation of this book.

Contents

You can find the answers to the Solve it! questions on page 45.

Some words are shown in bold, **like this**. You can find out what they mean by looking in the glossary on page 46.

What is an economy?

The economy is in the news almost every day. It affects you, and you affect it. Every country has an economy. What is this thing called the economy?

An economy is the way a country uses its **resources** to make, sell, and buy goods and services. Goods are things that are made, sold, and purchased. Services are things that one person pays another person to do. There are two parts to the definition of an economy – what a country has and how it uses what it has.

Copper is a natural resource that is taken from the ground, refined, and used to make goods such as electrical wiring and pipes. A copper mine in Utah is shown here.

In factories like this one in China, human resources (workers) use capital resources (tools and machines) to produce electronic goods.

Resources

Firstly, a country's economy is partly based on what resources it has available to use. There are three main types of resources. **Natural resources** include water, oil, soil, wood, precious stones, minerals, and coal. These **raw materials** can be **refined** and processed in order to make things. **Capital resources** include cash or property. Tools, machinery, and computers are examples of property used in manufacturing. **Human resources** are the people who use their skills, intelligence, and ideas in making, selling, and buying. When people buy things that are made, they are called **consumers**. Consumers are just as important as people who make or produce things. A country needs to have people who can buy the goods and services it produces.

Goods and services

Secondly, an economy involves what a country does with its resources. It is how a country uses its resources to produce and distribute goods and services. Goods are items people can buy, such as cars, shoes, or MP3 players. Services are activities that people pay someone else to do for them, such as cutting their hair, giving piano lessons, or mending a leaky tap.

Do all countries have the same economy?

Every country's **resource** supply is different. Some countries have many **natural resources**, such as oil. Some countries have few high-tech **capital resources**, such as computers. Some countries have **human resources** with higher-paying jobs and more money to spend.

Some countries have more capital resources than others. Japan, for example, has a lot of buildings, technology, and machinery to use in its economy.

Each country is also unique in how it uses its resources to make, buy, and sell goods and services. As a result, countries differ in the kinds and amounts of things they produce and sell.

Different economies, same problem

In spite of these differences, all economies face the same basic problem. People have unlimited needs and wants, and there are limited resources available to produce goods and services to satisfy those needs and wants. This problem is called **scarcity**. Because resources are scarce, or limited, each country must decide three things:

1. *What* goods and services should be made and how much?

2. *How* should those goods and services be made (using which resources)?

3. *Who* will consume, or buy, those goods and services?

The answers to these questions are determined by the type of **economic system** a country has.

Solve it!

Goods include food items you might buy. If you buy apples at a supermarket, you are buying a good that someone produced. Let's say you buy two kilograms of apples for £5, and you give the cashier a £20 note. How much change would you get? What are different combinations of notes that the cashier might give you?

Needs versus wants

Needs are the basic things that people require for survival, such as food and clothing.

Wants are the extras, such as a skateboard or jewellery.

What is an economic system?

Imagine you are a baker with a limited supply of baking resources. You must decide what to bake, knowing you will have to make a **trade-off**. When you choose to bake one thing, it means you will not have enough supplies, such as flour, to make something else.

Consumers experience opportunity cost, too. When you choose to eat at one restaurant, for example, the cost is missing out on another restaurant that you also like.

As a baker, you think it is important to give people a choice. So you use your resources to make a variety of breads and cakes. Because of scarcity, however, you can only make a few of each kind of bread and cookie. This is the **opportunity cost,** or the cost of choosing to make both breads and cakes, instead of making just one item. The cost of making a variety of baked goods is that you can only make a few of each type.

Your friend is also a baker. She thinks it is important to have a lot of her most popular item. She uses her resources to make dozens of cup cakes. She does not have enough flour left to make bread, but she is happy with this opportunity cost because she values amount over variety.

Nations are similar to these bakers. They decide how to use their resources based on what they think is important. The beliefs that guide these decisions make up a country's economic system. A country's economic system determines what products will be produced, how they will be produced, and who will consume them. Today, there are three main types of economic systems: free market, command, and socialist.

Economic systems

Free-market economies	Command economies	Socialist economies
value more individual freedom and less government interference.	value government-planned use of resources.	value both government planning and individual freedom.

What is a free-market economy?

A **free-market economy** is a type of **economic system**. It is also called free enterprise or **capitalism**. One central belief of this system is that private citizens may own **capital resources** such as machines and factories, and they may use the **profits** earned from this capital to satisfy their needs and wants. Another value is freedom of choice. Decisions about how **resources** are used are based on these beliefs.

Apple is a business in a free-market economy. The government does not tell Apple what goods to make. When Apple releases a new product, such as the iPhone, consumers are willing to queue and pay a lot of money in order to buy it.

Role of the government

In a free market, the government makes few economic decisions. The government does not plan or decide how businesses will use resources to produce goods and services. Instead, these decisions are made by sellers (people making things) and **consumers** (people buying things). Free-market systems are based on the idea that an economy works best if the government does not interfere. This principle is called **laissez-faire**, which is a French word meaning "leave alone".

Supply and demand

A free market works by the principle of **supply and demand**. Demand is what the consumers want or need and are willing and able to buy. Supply is the goods and services that sellers are willing and able to make in response to the demand.

In a free market, prices are linked to supply and demand. For example, if many people want the newest video game, demand is strong. Sellers know they can raise prices when demand is high, because people will pay more for that good. However, when the same game is older, demand goes down. When demand goes down, sellers have to lower prices in order to sell the game.

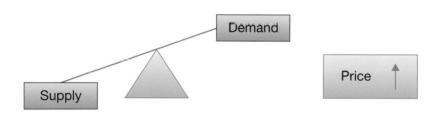

Demand | Supply | Price ↑ | When demand goes up, supply goes down. Seller can raise the price and consumers will pay.

Supply | Demand | Price ↓ | When demand goes down, supply goes up. Seller must lower price in order to sell.

Individual freedom

Freedom of choice is an important part of a free-market system. People can use their own capital resources to start a business to make and sell goods and services. These people are called **entrepreneurs**. Also, consumers can choose where to shop and how much to pay. If consumers do not like the goods or prices in one store, they can shop somewhere else. People are free to own their own property and sell it whenever they want.

Competition

A key feature of a free-market system is competition. For example, Katie can open a fruit smoothie shop down the street from Sam. Katie is free to sell the same kinds of smoothies as Sam. She can set her prices as high or low as she likes. If Katie wants to try to take business from Sam, she can make her prices lower than his. (Competition is strongest when entrepreneurs are free to enter markets when they think they can earn profits and leave markets when they lose money.)

Free-market economy

1. *What* should be made?	2. *How* should it be made?	3. *Who* should consume it?
Consumers determine which goods and services will be made. This is demand.	Businesses and entrepreneurs decide how they will meet the demand. This is supply.	People who work to pay for goods and services are the consumers.

Limits

There are limits to freedom in a free market. The government gets involved by creating laws and consequences for illegal economic activity. For example, everyone must pay taxes. Theft is illegal. A person cannot sell alcohol or cigarettes to under-aged customers.

If you go to a shopping centre, you will probably find more than one jewellers. These shops compete with each other to "win" customers. Competition is a key feature of the free-market system.

Advantages of a free-market economy

✓ Individuals are free to own property, start a business, and earn a profit from their hard work.

✓ There are many choices in a free market. Consumers are not limited to one bank or one type of shampoo.

✓ The government stays out of private business. It does not tell people what to make or how to make it.

Disadvantages of a free-market economy

✗ A free market is more risky because businesses are not guaranteed success. For example, entrepreneurs might lose a lot of money if they cannot sell their product or service.

✗ Because there is competition, there might be only one "winner". A big company such as Tesco can offer more choices and lower prices than a small shop opened by an entrepreneur. If consumers stop shopping at the small shop because they can get better deals at Tesco, the small shop will eventually go **bankrupt**.

✗ There is often a big gap between rich and poor. People who work hard or who have more education or ideas earn more money because these abilities are valuable in a free market. People with fewer ideas, less education, or abilities that are not in demand are paid less and thus may end up poor.

Entrepreneurs in a free market can sell goods and services online, too.

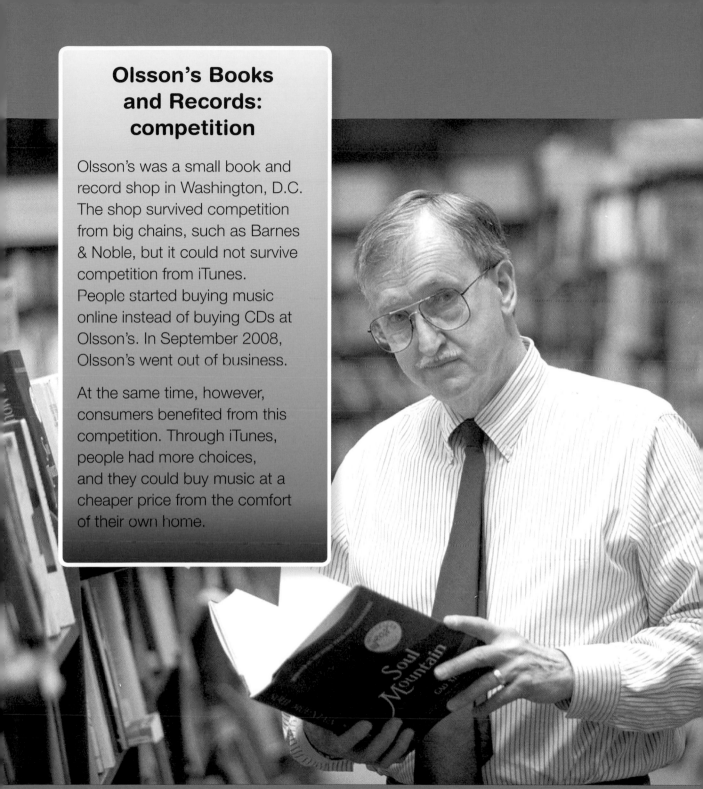

Olsson's Books and Records: competition

Olsson's was a small book and record shop in Washington, D.C. The shop survived competition from big chains, such as Barnes & Noble, but it could not survive competition from iTunes. People started buying music online instead of buying CDs at Olsson's. In September 2008, Olsson's went out of business.

At the same time, however, consumers benefited from this competition. Through iTunes, people had more choices, and they could buy music at a cheaper price from the comfort of their own home.

Which countries have a free-market economy?

No country today has a completely **free-market economy**. The government often has some influence in economic decisions. There are several countries, however, that are mostly run under free-market principles such as **supply and demand**. Three examples are Japan, the United Kingdom, and the United States.

Japan

As of 2009, Japan had the fourth-largest economy in the world. This means that Japan is using its **resources** wisely to make and sell goods and services.

Japan does not have many **natural resources**. For example, it has poor soil, so there is not much farming. However, Japan does have a lot of **capital resources**, such as technology and computers, and many **human resources** who can use that technology. As a result, Japan is an industrialized country. This means most of the country's resources are used in making things.

People in Tokyo, Japan, are paid some of the highest **wages** in the world. These **consumers** are able to buy the expensive, high-tech goods that Japanese businesses produce, such as electronics and cars.

Flow of money in the economy

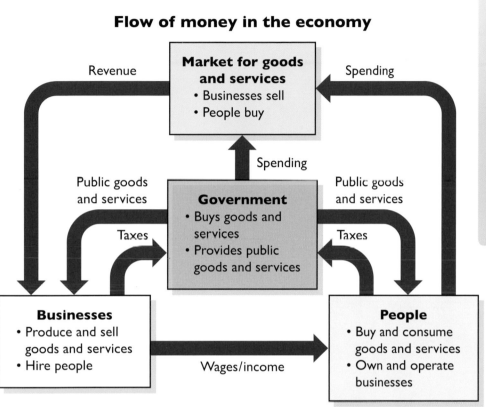

This flowchart shows how a free-market economy works. **Revenue** refers to income. Public goods and services refer to things the government provides using money from taxes. These include the health service, national defence, street lighting, road repairs, etc.

Economy size

Economy size is measured by **gross domestic product (GDP)**. GDP is the value of all goods and services produced in a country in one year. A higher GDP means a country is using its resources effectively and producing a lot. A lower GDP usually means a country is poor. This could be because the country is not using its resources effectively or that it has limited resources to work with.

The world's largest economy

The United States has the largest economy in the world. Its GDP, or total goods and services made in a year, is over $14 trillion. In this free market, business owners and entrepreneurs decide what to make and how to use available resources. They make some very advanced technology, such as equipment for medical, aerospace, and military uses. Both the national government and individual state governments buy goods and services from these businesses.

United Kingdom

As of 2009, the United Kingdom had the seventh-largest economy in the world. About 75 per cent, or three-quarters, of the United Kingdom's gross domestic product (GDP) comes from services, not goods. These services include financial (banking), transport, and hotels. Businesses in the United Kingdom have used available human resources and capital resources to meet this demand for services. **Entrepreneurs**, for example, have opened hotels and sightseeing tours because a lot of peole come to the United Kingdom on holiday.

Housing bubble: supply and demand

Between 2000 and 2006, banks were charging low **interest** rates to borrow money. This made it easy for people to get a **mortgage** to buy a house. As a result, the demand for houses went up, and so did the price. Demand and prices kept rising until the bubble "burst".This happened when the low interest rates suddenly increased, and people could not afford the mortgage repayments on their home. Many people stopped paying the banks back. The banks took these houses and tried to resell them. Now there was an increased supply of houses. At the same time, it became harder to borrow money. The demand for houses dropped, and so did the prices.

What is a command economy?

Another type of **economic system** is a **command economy**. This system is also known as a planned economy or **communism**. The beliefs that guide a command system are very different from the ones that guide a free market. As a result, the decisions communist countries make about how to use **resources** and how to distribute what is produced are very different from the decisions made in free-market societies.

Role of the government

A command economy is the opposite of a **free-market economy**. The government mostly stays out of the free-market system and lets the laws of **supply and demand** determine products and prices. In a command system, however, the government plans the country's economy. The government decides how to use the country's resources and what to make with those resources. This economic system values equality, so the government takes control to make sure everyone is taken care of and that there is no division between rich and poor.

Lack of freedom

In a true command system, all property and businesses are owned by the government. People cannot become **entrepreneurs**. They are not free to start a business and make a **profit** from it. The government decides which businesses are needed and who will run them, and evenly distributes the profits.

Public versus private

Publicly owned businesses belong to the government.	*Privately owned* businesses belong to individuals.

Because the government makes the economic decisions in a command system, people do not have a say in what is produced. **Consumers** generally have fewer options to choose from.

Co-operation, not competition

In a free-market society, people can compete for jobs or open a store just like the one down the street. In a **command economy**, the government emphasizes cooperation, not competition. The government decides what jobs are available and what the **wages** will be. The government also sets prices on things that are made and sold. There is no competition between businesses because all businesses are owned by the government and have the same products and prices.

	Free-market economy	Command economy
What is the government's role?	makes few decisions	makes all decisions
Does the system run by co-operation or competition?	competition	co-operation
Which principle guides the economy: central planning or supply and demand?	supply and demand	central planning
Who owns property and businesses?	individuals	the government
Does the system emphasise individual freedom?	yes	no

Free-market and command economies are based on opposite values and beliefs.

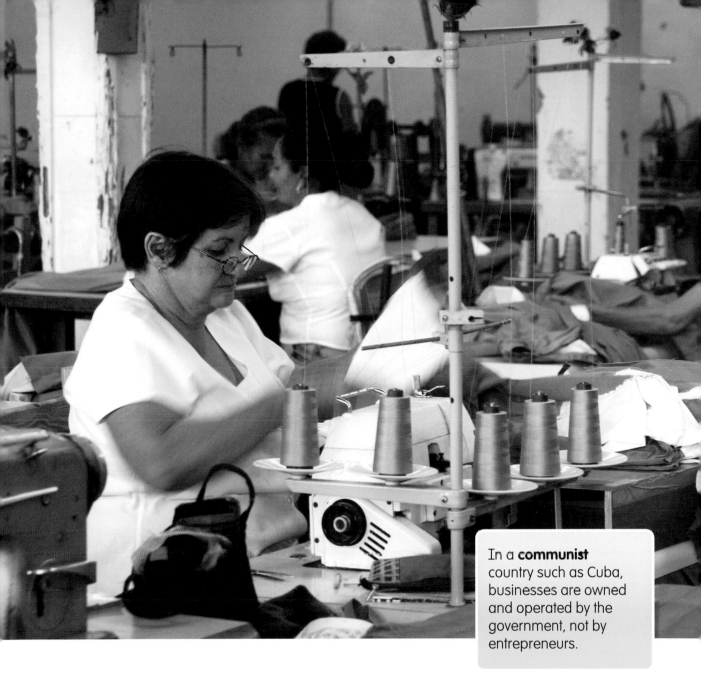

In a **communist** country such as Cuba, businesses are owned and operated by the government, not by entrepreneurs.

Solve it!

Based on what you have read, can you think of one advantage of living in a country with a command economy? Can you think of one disadvantage? Write down your answers before you turn the page.

Advantages of a command economy

✓ Since a command economy is centrally planned by the government, it may be more stable. This means there is less risk of people losing their jobs.

✓ The government uses money from taxes to provide services such as health care and education so that everyone is taken care of, not just people who can afford to buy these things.

✓ There is more equality in incomes and wealth because the government sets wages and evenly distributes its property.

Command economy

1. *What* should be made?	2. *How* should it be made?	3. *Who* should consume it?
The government decides what will be made and how much. The result is a limited number of choices for the consumer.	The government decides which company will make the goods and services and which resources will be used.	The government decides who needs it and how much consumers will pay.

Disadvantages of a command economy

✗ People have very few choices when they buy goods and services. The government might produce only one type of good, and the consumer has little input into what is produced.

✗ People are not motivated to work hard. If workers know they cannot earn more money by extra effort, what is the point of doing more than they need to?

✗ There is no individual freedom of choice. A person cannot choose to start a new business or buy a home or change jobs.

One value of a command economy is equality. Using tax money, the government provides the same education and health care to everyone.

Which countries have a command economy?

Before 1991, there were more than 30 countries with a **command economy**. Examples included the Soviet Union, Romania, and Hungary. Over time, most of these countries have decreased the amount of government control and have introduced free-market ideas. Today, there are only two countries in which the government makes most, if not all, economic decisions: Cuba and North Korea.

Cuba

This island country is located south of Florida. Cuba's government is run by General Raul Castro, who took over from his brother, Fidel Castro, in 2008.

Cuba is a **communist** country. The government owns the property and businesses that produce the country's goods and services.

Most Cubans have a poor **standard of living**. This is partly because the government sets their **wages** very low and partly because the government does not use its **resources** to make **luxuries** for people to buy and enjoy, such as air conditioners and DVD players.

In February 2008, Raul Castro started taking steps to improve Cuba's economy. These steps include increasing wages, allowing some Cubans to own their homes, and letting people buy goods such as mobile phones, computers, and microwaves, which were previously owned by very few. Also, a small number of people are being allowed to work for a **profit**. For example, hairstylists and people who run small restaurants from their homes are being allowed to set their own prices.

Many Cubans work on **communal** farms, or farms that are owned by groups of people. The government determines how much money people earn for this work.

North Korea

The best example of a command economy today can be found in North Korea. This country is located between China and South Korea. Kim Jong-il has ruled North Korea since 1997.

North Korea's government plans every aspect of the country's economy. The government owns all businesses and property, and it makes all decisions regarding production, prices, and wages. Because the government wants the people to be equal in every way, it provides housing, health care, and education to everyone. The government even gives people the same amount of food through food **rations**.

Because of scarcity, all countries must make a **trade-off**. North Korea, for example, spends most of its resources on its armed forces, knowing that there will not be money left to produce luxuries that people can buy and enjoy.

Because of its location, North Korea does not have many **natural resources** available to make goods and services. It has a lot of steep mountains, and the soil is not good for farming. The country also has few **capital resources** such as cash and computers. Due to this **scarcity**, the government has to decide what to do with the resources it has. The North Korean government has chosen to spend a lot of money on building up its military strength. As a result, there is not much left over to improve the standard of living for the people. The government is happy with this **opportunity cost** because it values having strong armed forces.

Censorship

One result of a controlled economy is **censorship**, or restricting access to information. The North Korean government limits the production and sale of goods and services such as the internet and mobile phones. This means most people do not have access to email, websites, or other information from the world outside their country. People do not have the freedom to sell, shop, or look for a job online.

What is socialism?

Think about **economic systems** as being dots on a straight line. At one end is the command system, or **communism**, and at the other end is the free market, or **capitalism**. They are opposites. In the middle is a third type of economic system called **socialism**, which has features of the other two systems. In socialist countries, government planning and free-market competition both determine how **resources** are used to make, buy, and sell goods and services.

Command features

As in a **command economy**, the government in socialist countries has a big role in economic decisions. For example, the government controls many important areas such as health care, energy, and public transport. By owning businesses in these areas, the government can decide what is produced and who should receive the goods and services. The government also determines fair **wages** and sets prices for some products.

In addition, socialism shares the command economy values of equality and co-operation. The government uses tax money to give everyone equal access to health care, education, and other essential needs.

Vietnam: A case where socialism has succeeded

Vietnam used to be a closed communist country with a command economy. In 1986, the government started introducing free-market ideas such as letting individuals own businesses. Today, Vietnam's economy is more socialist, with both government and individuals making decisions about how to use resources. As a result, Vietnam's **gross domestic product** has grown, people are earning higher wages, and **poverty** has decreased.

Free-market features

Like a **free-market economy**, socialism allows for private ownership of property and businesses. While the government controls some industries such as transport, **entrepreneurs** can open restaurants, cinemas, car showrooms, and many other businesses. The people who own these companies can decide what to make and how much to charge. They can try to make a **profit** and increase their personal wealth. This allows for some competition in the economy, and the laws of **supply and demand** have some influence in setting prices.

Even in the government-owned businesses of socialist economies, managers are given more decision-making power than they are in command economies. Managers might be able to hire and fire employees, as well as give a worker an increase in wages if he or she has earned it.

Venezuela: A case where socialism has failed

Under the guidance of President Hugo Chavez, Venezuela has become more socialist by increasing government control. Since the mid-2000s, the government has taken over many important industries, including petroleum (oil), tourism, and banking. As a result, the number of privately-owned businesses has decreased and so has free-market competition. The **standard of living** for many people has decreased. People have experienced a loss of individual freedoms as well as shortages of food and energy.

Advantages of socialism

✓ The government can provide some regulations and laws to make production and distribution of goods and services effective.

✓ The government can provide schemes and services to help the whole population, including the poor, who might not be able to pay for those services in a free-market economy.

✓ Individuals still have the freedom to start their own business and make a profit.

Socialism

1. *What* should be made?	2. *How* should it be made?	3. *Who* should consume it?
Both government and entrepreneurs decide what will be made.	Both government and entrepreneurs decide what resources will be used.	The government decides in some cases, as when it provides university education or health care. In other cases, the **consumer** is willing to work for goods.

Disadvantages of socialism

✗ In order to pay for public services such as education and **pensions**, the government takes money out of its citizens' wages. These taxes are very high, sometimes 50 to 60 per cent of a person's income.

✗ If communism is dominant, people might have fewer freedoms. If capitalism is dominant, there might be more risk of people losing their jobs.

✗ With free-market competition, there is the potential for a big gap between rich and poor. People who work hard or who have more ideas earn higher wages than people who have abilities that are not in demand.

Denmark has a socialist economy. People who live there enjoy a higher standard of living and many government-provided services. However, they also pay the highest taxes in the world.

Which countries have a socialist economy?

Today, approximately ten countries practice **socialism**. Three examples are included here: Sweden, Norway, and China. Sweden and Norway have based economic decisions on socialism for several decades. China, on the other hand, used to have a strict **command economy** and has recently become more socialist.

Sweden

Scandinavia is a region in northern Europe made up of five countries, the largest of which is Sweden. This country has effectively used socialism to give its citizens one of the highest **standards of living** in the world.

In Sweden's **socialist economy**, the government owns the industries that provide **benefits** such as child care, retirement **pensions**, and time off when a person is ill. The government spends a large percentage of tax money on health care in particular. As a result, Sweden has one of the highest ranking health care systems in the world, and the benefits are available to everyone. (For advantages and disadvantages of government-provided health care, look at the boxes on pages 37 and 38.)

Sweden also has a strong free market. The country is rich in **human resources** . Many are skilled workers, who use their **capital resources** to start businesses. Privately-owned businesses produce approximately 90 per cent of Sweden's manufactured goods.

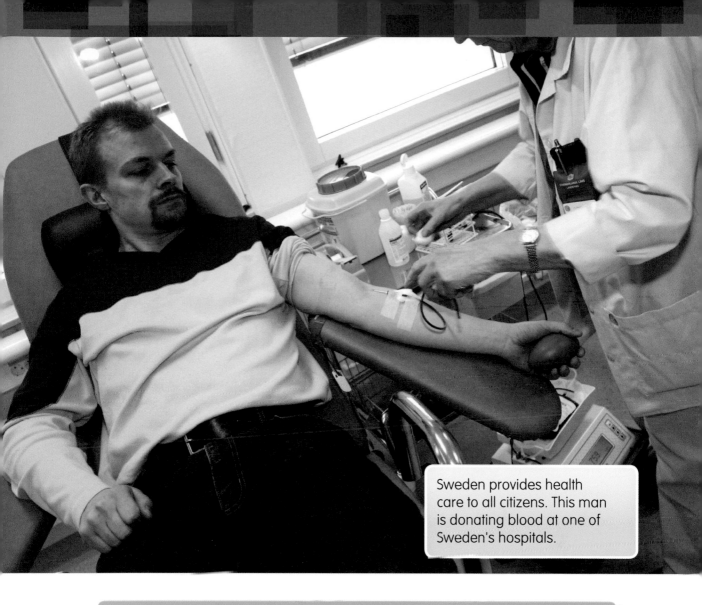

Sweden provides health care to all citizens. This man is donating blood at one of Sweden's hospitals.

Government-controlled health care: advantages

✓ Everyone has equal access to doctors and medicines.

✓ If the government spends a lot of money on health care, people will probably have access to advanced medical technology and well-trained doctors.

Norway

Another country with a successful **socialist economy** is Norway, which is located next to Sweden, in Scandinavia. Norway is one of the richest nations in the world in terms of **gross domestic product** divided by the number of citizens. As of 2009, Norway ranked 5th in the world, higher than the United Kingdom (34th) and the United States (11th).

Norway is rich in **natural resources** such as petroleum (oil), fish, and forests. Norway's government has effectively used these resources to make money, or **revenue**, and to strengthen the economy. The government controls several key industries, including oil and natural gas. The petroleum industry makes up 30 per cent of the state revenue. With this money from oil, Norway has expanded its social welfare programmes, which provide hospital care, dental plans, and pensions for use after retirement.

People in Norway have the freedom to become **entrepreneurs** and earn a **profit** from their businesses. As a result, people have a lot of capital resources and enjoy a high standard of living.

Government-controlled health care: disadvantages

✗ As everyone has equal access, there are very long waiting times to see a doctor.

✗ The government decides how much it will pay for medicines. If the price is too high, the government may choose a less expensive, and possibly less effective, medicine. In order to maintain equality, the government may also prevent people from buying the more expensive medicine on their own.

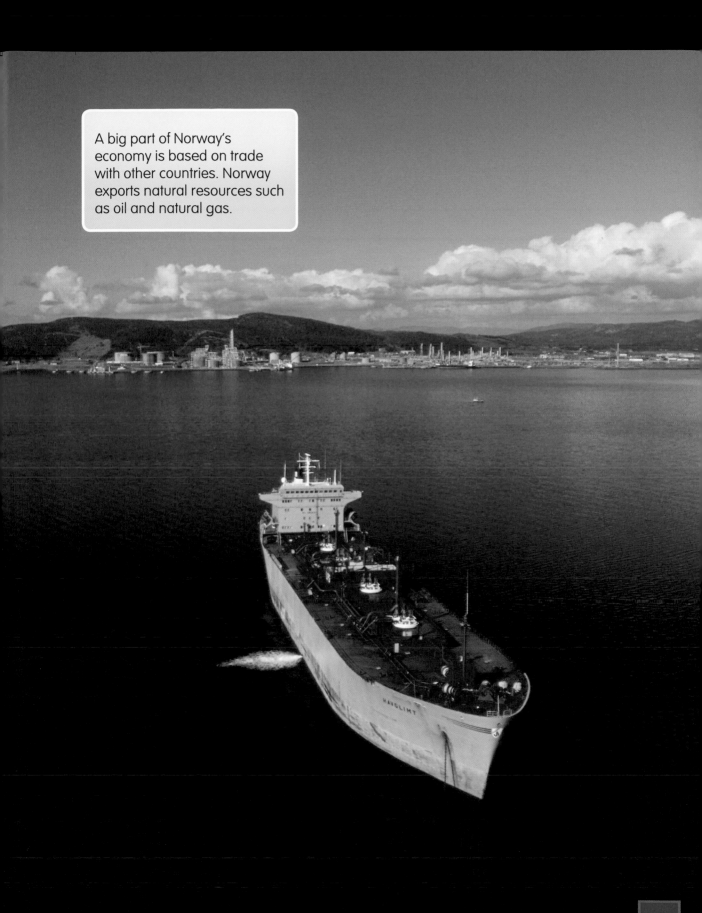

A big part of Norway's economy is based on trade with other countries. Norway exports natural resources such as oil and natural gas.

One out of every five people in the world lives in China!

China

From 1949 to 1978, China was a **communist** country with a **command economy**. Though the communist party is still in power, China's economy has changed a lot. It is now considered socialist, with both government control and private ownership.

In 1979, the government started applying free-market ideas. It broke up the **communal** farms (farms that were owned by groups of people.) The government then gave individual families their own farms, and families were able to keep their profits.

The government also started giving more control to managers of government-owned companies. For the first time, people started receiving pay increases based on how hard they worked. These changes have continued for over 30 years, and many people no longer live in **poverty**. China now has the third-largest economy in the world.

In some economic decisions, China's communist government has more control than the governments of most socialist countries. For example, the Chinese government tells website companies to create jobs for people who will **censor**, or limit, material published online. In this way, the government controls what people can read on the internet. In addition, each couple is allowed to have only one child. (There is controversy that surrounds this law, though. And, it doesn't apply to all Chinese couples.) China has this limit to control population growth. A bigger population means a bigger problem of **scarcity**, or more wants and needs than can be met by China's limited resources.

Solve it!

Based on what you have read, which do you think is best: a free-market economy, a command economy, or socialism? List reasons why.

IN FOCUS:

What money is used around the world?

Each country has its own economy and its own money, or **currency**. Many countries use the dollar ($) as their currency. Can you guess which countries use the dollar by looking at the flags below and on the opposite page?

You can find the answers on page 45.

Other countries use different currencies. See if you can match the country to its currency. You can find the answers on page 45.

China	yen
Cuba	pound
Germany	rupee
India	peso
Israel	shilling
Japan	yúan
Kenya	shekel
Saudi Arabia	euro*
United Kingdom	riyal

*As of January 2009, 16 European countries use the euro. They are Austria, Belgium, Cyprus, Finland, France, Greece, Ireland, Italy, Luxembourg, Malta, the Netherlands, Portugal, Slovakia, Slovenia, Spain, and one of the countries in the table above.

Summary

Every country in the world has an economy. **Gross domestic product (GDP)** measures the strength of a country's economy. The dollar amount is the value of all goods and services produced within a nation in one year. A higher GDP means the country is using its **resources** effectively to make a lot of products. It also means the country has **consumers** who have **capital resources** to buy what is produced. A lower GDP means either the country is not using its resources effectively, or the country has very limited **natural**, capital, or **human resources** to work with.

Look at the graph below to compare the 2009 GDP for the countries discussed in this book. Notice that the last two countries, Cuba and North Korea, are quite a bit lower than all the others.

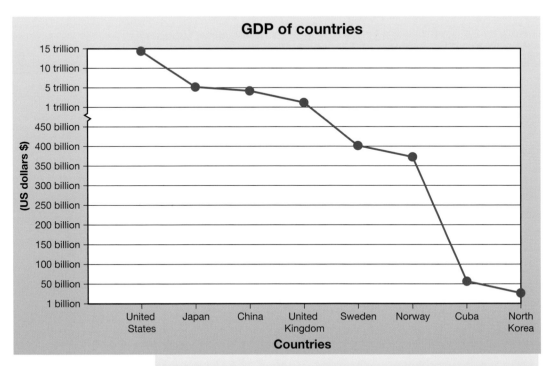

The values in this graph are taken from the CIA World Factbook.

Answers to Solve it! and currency quizzes

page 7:
You will receive £15 in change. Some combinations are: one £10 note and one £5 note, *or* one £10 note and five £1 notes, *or* three £5 notes, *or* two £5 notes and five $1 notes, *or* one £5 and ten £1notes, *or* fifteen £1 bills.

page 23:
See pages 24–25 for several advantages and disadvantages.

page 42:
1. Hong Kong, 2. Canada 3. New Zealand 4. United States 5. Australia

page 43:
China = yúan, Cuba = peso, Germany = euro, India = rupee, Israel = shekel, Japan = yen, Kenya = shilling, Saudi Arabia = riyal, United Kingdom = pound. Germany also uses the Euro.

Glossary

bankrupt run out of money and unable to pay bills

benefis can be any good or helpful outcome from an action. In the economy, it means extra things provided, such as pensions

capital resource asset or property that can be used to make and sell goods and services; examples include cash and technology

capitalism type of economic system that values private ownership, competition, and little government involvement; another name for free market

censor limit access to information

command economy type of economic system that values government-planned economic activities; also known as communism

communal shared, owned, or participated in as a group

communism type of political and economic system that values co-operation and communal ownership of property

consumer person who buys and uses goods and services

currency coins and banknotes used as money in a country

economic system beliefs and values that guide a country's economic decisions

entrepreneur person who starts a business

free-market economy type of economic system that values private ownership, competition, and little government involvement; also called capitalism and free enterprise

gross domestic product (GDP) value of all goods and services made in a country in one year; amount is given in US dollars

human resources supply of human skills, intelligence, and ideas used to make and sell good and services; includes consumers

interest amount of money that is paid in return for money borrowed, for example from a bank. The interest rate affects the percentage of the loan that has to be repaid each month.

laissez-faire idea that the government should not interfere with economic activity

luxury an extra; something comforting and enjoyable but not needed for survival

mortgage money lent for a certain amount of time and at a certain fee to help buy a house

natural resource raw materials that occur in nature and can be used to make and sell goods and services; examples include oil, coal, and natural gas

opportunity cost "cost" of choosing one opportunity over another; cost is based on what is given up when making a decision

pension fixed amount paid to someone, usually after that person retires from a job

poverty not having basic needs met

profit money earned after subtracting expenses

ration same, limited amount of something, such as food, given to all people

raw material material that can be processed and refined into a different, more usable form

refine to purify and make useable

resource something that can be used to make and sell goods and services

revenue money earned before subtracting expenses

scarcity in economic terms, problem of having limited resources to meet unlimited wants and needs

socialism type of economic system that values both

public (government) and private (individual) control of economic decisions

socialist economy *see* socialism

standard of living level of necessities and luxuries enjoyed in everyday life

supply and demand basic principle behind free-market economy; idea that prices are set by the relationship between demand (what consumers want) and supply (the goods and services produced to meet the demand)

trade-off giving up one thing in exchange for something else; results in an opportunity cost

wages money paid to workers; money earned by workers

Find out more

Books

A Kid's Guide to the Economy (Money Matters: A Kid's Guide to the Economy), Tamra Orr (Mitchell Lane Publishers, 2010)

Capitalism (Political and Economic Systems), David Downing (Heinemann Library 2009)

Graphing Money, Patrick Catel (Heinemann Library, 2010).

Websites

www.socialstudiesforkids.com/subjects/economics.htm
This website has information on basic economics, including supply and demand, scarcity, wants versus needs, and more.

www.cia.gov/library/publications/the-world-factbook/index.html
The *CIA World Factbook* has information and statistics about every country in tho world.

news.bbc.co.uk/2/hi/country_profiles/default.stm
The BBC website has historical, political, and economic information on every country in the world. You can search the profiles by continent, country, and territory.

Index